Appli-QUILTING
Appliqué & Quilt at the Same Time!

SKILL-BUILDING PROJECTS

TECHNIQUES FOR
ALL MACHINES

Gina Perkes

C&T PUBLISHING

Publisher: Amy Marson

Creative Director: Gailen Runge

Editors: Lynn Koolish and
Katie Van Amburg

Technical Editors:
Alison M. Schmidt and
Deanna Csomo McCool

Cover/Book Designer: Page + Pixel

Production Coordinator:
Zinnia Heinzmann

Production Editors:
Jennifer Warren, Nicole Rolandelli,
and Alice Mace Nakanishi

Illustrator:
Kirstie L. Pettersen

Photo Assistant:
Carly Jean Marin

Instructional photography
by Diane Pedersen, unless
otherwise noted

Published by C&T Publishing, Inc., P.O. Box 1456, Lafayette, CA 94549

Library of Congress Cataloging-in-Publication Data

Names: Perkes, Gina, 1974- author.

Title: Appli-quilting--appliqué & quilt at the same time! : skill-building
projects - techniques for all machines / Gina Perkes.

Description: Lafayette, CA : C&T Publishing, Inc., 2016.

Identifiers: LCCN 2016018782 | ISBN 9781617452741 (soft cover)

Subjects: LCSH: Appliqué--Patterns. | Machine quilting--Patterns.

Classification: LCC TT779 .P46 2016 | DDC 746.44/5--dc23

LC record available at https://lccn.loc.gov/2016018782

Printed in China

10 9 8 7 6 5 4 3 2 1

Dedication

This book is dedicated to my beautiful daughter,
Rylie. She adds color and sparkle to my world
with her radiant energy. She is my only daughter,
my first-born child, my best friend, and my
inspiration!

Acknowledgments

Thank you to my students for your enthusiasm
for the Appli-Quilting technique!

A big thank-you to C&T Publishing for working
with me on this project and publishing amazing
resources for quilters! I'd like to especially thank
Lynn Koolish, my developmental editor, who
provided patience and guidance through new,
uncharted territory (a book with projects).

Thank you to my support system: Kathy Hunt,
Debbie Vaughn, Arleen Logan, and Felicia Brenoe.
You are always willing to help at the eleventh hour,
testing patterns, cutting, pressing, gluing down
appliqué shapes, and speed binding. You are all
amazing women whom I love and cherish!

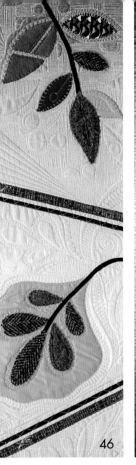

CONTENTS

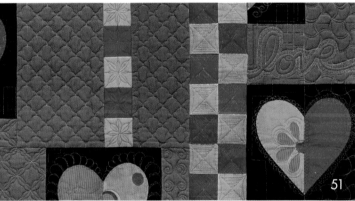

Introduction

Early in my career, I was very fortunate to meet Linda V. Taylor, an amazing woman, quilter, and pioneer in the longarm quilting industry. She was incredibly encouraging to me, and I am so thankful for the confidence that she helped me to build.

I was quite new to the world of show quilting and hadn't even begun to teach when Linda invited me to be a guest on her show *Linda's Longarm Quilting*. I was completely honored and extremely scared. What could I possibly have to teach other longarm quilters? I thought, experimented, and played at my machine, trying to develop a novel concept using my longarm machine.

Blanket stitching and couching on a longarm were born! For more than a decade, I have developed the Appli-Quilting technique, and now I teach it throughout the country. I am pleased that it is every bit as fun and easy using a longarm as it is using a home sewing machine.

My favorite thing about this book is that it combines two popular and amazing techniques—appliquéing and quilting—providing extremely versatile and interpretive techniques with endless possibilities. I hope that you enjoy learning Appli-Quilting and creating pieces either from the book or from your imagination! I encourage you to apply your own creative twists to my technique, using your own unique versions of the stitches and designs. Allow yourself to become lost in your happy, quilty world. Remember, quilting is cheaper than therapy!

How to Use This Book

Machine Requirements

Appli-Quilting can be beautifully executed on any style of machine. The only machine requirements are that the feed dogs can be disengaged and the machine can perform a single stitch. I have used Appli-Quilting with both longarm and domestic machines, computerized and noncomputerized. Throughout this book, I have included tips for both longarm and domestic machine styles. Appli-Quilting is based not on what your machine is capable of but on what you can create with your own imagination and skills. Always remember: It's not the violin; it's the violinist.

Longarm versus Domestic Sewing Machines

LONGARM

When I refer to a *longarm* machine, I am referring to a quilting machine that is attached to a track system. With this style of machine, the quilt is loaded onto the frame rather than sandwiched. The machines themselves are quite simple. Once the quilt is loaded, the quilter moves the machine over the quilt to create quilting designs. The quilt remains stationary. Longarm machines do not have feed dogs; the quilting is always free motion. These machines are only capable of straight stitching. The operator is the one who produces the designs by guiding the machine.

DOMESTIC

When I refer to a *domestic*, or *home*, machine, I am referring to a sit-down style of home sewing machine. Sit-down longarm (and mid-arm) machines are also becoming quite popular. This style of machine is stationary and is mounted to a cabinet or table. With these machines, the designs are created by moving the quilt sandwich beneath the stationary machine. The quilt layers should be sandwiched ahead of time.

For Appli-Quilting, you don't use the feed dogs or computerized/built-in stitches. The machine should be in its simplest form: feed dogs disengaged and a straight stitch selected with the stitch width set at zero. The stitch length doesn't matter; it will be determined by how fast or slowly you move the fabric. Though a stitch regulator may be used to keep the stitch length consistent, it is not required or necessary.

Choosing Your Methods and Fabrics

The Appli-Quilting technique can be used with any appliqué project, including those in this book (see Projects, page 45). After you have selected a project, decide on a method or combination of methods, as discussed in Preparing the Shapes (page 11). Select your fabrics based on the method or methods you plan to use; certain fabrics work best with certain methods. The patterns are all easily translatable based on your preferences and style. I encourage you to make the designs your own and have fun in the process!

Choosing Your Stitches

There are no limits on the stitch designs that can be created with Appli-Quilting. Stitches (page 27) features a wide variety of both traditional and nontraditional stitch designs. You may wish to use a variety in one project or stick with just one or two. You have the creative license to choose whichever stitches you think fit your quilt.

Creating the Quilt Sandwich

After your appliqué designs have been prepared and tacked in place, prepare your quilt sandwich using your preferred basting or pinning method. If you are using a longarm machine, load the three layers onto the machine. At this point your appliqué shapes are not stitched down, only tacked temporarily. The shapes are stitched down with the quilting using Appli-Quilting.

Fabric Selection

Texture feeds your sense of touch.

Any fabric may be used for raw-edge appliqué, though nonraveling fabrics are my preferred choice because the stitches discussed in the following chapters are fairly open. Unlike dense satin stitching, which secures the fabric's edges within the stitches, open stitch designs leave the fabric edges somewhat exposed. These uncovered edges can begin to ravel or fray over time.

When used for raw-edge appliqué, the following fabrics add a special element to your designs: texture! Most quilters fall in love not only with the visual appeal of quiltmaking but with the process of working in a tactile medium. Introducing textured fabrics into your world feeds your sense of touch, adding to the joy of quilting.

Ultrasuede

Ultrasuede is a beautiful fabric with many unique characteristics. In the 1980s and early 1990s, Ultrasuede was popular in the fashion industry and was often used by garment sewers. These days it's less commonly used in garments, though it has become quite popular in the home decor industry. I have been using Ultrasuede in my quilts for more than fifteen years. I love the sophisticated touch that it adds to my appliqué designs. Though it is a very expensive fabric ($30–$60 per yard), small doses can have a large impact. I like to use it mainly for the appliqué shapes, combining it with less expensive background fabrics. The following are some of the qualities that make this fabric an appealing choice for raw-edge appliqué.

UNIQUE TEXTURE

Ultrasuede provides a unique texture that adds life to appliqué shapes. It has a suedelike texture with a subtle nap. There is no wrong side, though one side generally has more nap than the other. Pay attention to which side you use as the right side if you'd like the texture to remain consistent throughout.

Fractured Leaves

DOESN'T RAVEL

Ultrasuede does not ravel at all, making it an excellent choice for raw-edge appliqué projects. It is especially good to use instead of turned-edge techniques for small cut-out details and sharp points.

Compare the photographs (below). Both designs use the raw-edge method (page 13) with open stitch designs.

Detail of *Smitten* (page 51). This example uses a cotton fabric prone to fraying.

Detail of *Fractured Leaves* (at left). This example showcases Ultrasuede fabric, which does not fray or ravel.

CAN BE DIE CUT

A variety of cutting machines on the market provide a quick, accurate way to cut fabrics for quilting. Some pattern designers include files with their patterns formatted for cutting machines. I have found that these machines cut Ultrasuede even better than they cut most cotton fabrics. I prefer to use a die-cut machine, particularly when I use intricate designs with elaborate cutwork.

Detail of *Winter Wonderland* pillow. Some patterns are quite elaborate, with intricate cutwork. A cutting machine is a great tool for these types of designs.

VARIETY

Several different varieties of Ultrasuede are available. They vary in weight and are offered in a large assortment of colors. Ultrasuede is typically found in solid colors; prints are uncommon.

Ultrasuede comes in a wide array of beautiful colors.

Based on your appliqué design, experiment with different weights. If you plan to overlap or stack pieces, choose a variety that is more lightweight. Multiple layers of heavy Ultrasuede can be difficult to stitch through, especially when sandwiched for quilting.

Ultrasuede is available in several different weights.

EASY TO CARE FOR

Even with its lavish visual appeal and texture, Ultrasuede can be machine washed. I typically avoid drying it in a dryer, opting instead to hang it to air-dry. Avoid pressing directly onto Ultrasuede with a hot iron—it destroys the fabric. If pressing is necessary, use a pressing cloth and an iron set to a low heat setting. Always perform a test before working on your actual project.

Avoid using a hot iron with Ultrasuede.

Felted Wool

Felted wool lends itself amazingly well to raw-edge appliqué. It is quite versatile stylistically and is available in many colors and patterns. Hand-dyed felted wool is gorgeous and can add a dynamic visual impact to your projects. Like Ultrasuede, it is pricey, but small pieces can provide a significant impact!

HOW TO FELT YOUR OWN WOOL

Has one of your wool garments ever accidentally worked its way into a load of laundry? If so, chances are you ended up with a miniature version—with a very different texture. Congratulations! You felted wool! Most of us have experienced this at one time or another. Wool fibers are prone to a high degree of shrinkage activated by hot water and agitation. When this shrinkage occurs, the fibers become felted. To intentionally felt 100% wool, simply wash and dry the fabric using high heat. Sometimes I repeat the felting process two or three times until the edges no longer fray when cut.

This piece of fabric is still fraying a bit and would benefit from another felting cycle.

After two more felting cycles, the edges are no longer raveling and the fabric is ready to use.

TIP: Treasure Hunting for Ultrasuede and Wool

Because Ultrasuede and felted wool tend to be expensive, I always look for bargains and unexpected places to purchase these types of fabrics. It is surprisingly easy to find garments constructed of wool or Ultrasuede in secondhand stores or even at yard sales. Many folks clean out their closets and part with garments that have overstayed their welcome. I have purchased skirts and jackets constructed with Ultrasuede and wool for less than a dollar. These garments often yield more than two yards of usable fabric. Once I bring my finds home, they pay a visit or two to the washing machine. When they are thoroughly cleaned, they are ready for the deconstruction and upcycling process. Treasure hunting is a great way to find bargains and spectacular fabrics for your projects without breaking your budget.

Secondhand garments can be upcycled into beautiful projects without breaking the budget.

Felt

Wool felt and felt blends, such as rayon or bamboo felt, are a great choice for raw-edge appliqué. These types of fabrics do not ravel and are easy to find in fabric and craft stores. One major benefit is that they are much more affordable than Ultrasuede and felted wool while still offering unique texture and nonraveling edges. I often choose felts for projects that have a utilitarian function.

Wool felt and felt blends are inexpensive and readily available fabric choices for raw-edge appliqué designs.

Leather

Leather is another unique material that can be used in Appli-Quilting. It doesn't ravel, which makes it a great choice for raw-edge techniques. It is a bit expensive but can be quite effective in small doses. Remember to increase the size of your needle and use a heavier thread when quilting over leather.

Fabrics That Fray

You may wish to use nonspecialty fabrics, including quilting cottons, that may be prone to raveling and fraying. Some quilters like the look of fraying edges. For fabrics that fray, I like to use the fusible method (page 17) for preparing the appliqué shapes. Fusibles help reduce fraying somewhat and provide stability to the appliqué shapes.

TIP: Fraying Effect

To accentuate the fraying effect, stitch away from the edge and then snip the fabric up to the stitching line.

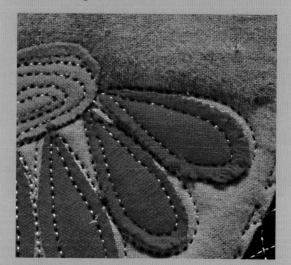

Accentuating the fraying effect

Preparing the Shapes

With Appli-Quilting, you can use any pattern or method for preparing your shapes. The technique is extremely versatile and open to interpretation. As you experiment and learn the different methods, it will become easier for you to determine which method is most appropriate for your particular project. I always consider style and function first and foremost.

There are many techniques for preparing appliqué shapes. Different techniques yield different effects.

Some methods, such as raw-edge appliqué, are fairly quick, while others, such as turned-edge appliqué, are more time consuming. Remember that there are no quilting police: You are free to choose the methods that produce the effects you desire based on the style and function of your particular project.

Discussed in this chapter are three popular machine appliqué techniques: raw-edge (page 13), turned-edge (page 13), and fusible (page 17).

Supplies

- Lightbox (see Using a Lightbox, at right)

- Good scissors for fabric

- Not-as-good scissors for paper or template plastic

- Erasable marking implements for light- and dark-colored fabrics

- Appliqué template plastic

- Fusible web (*for the fusible method*)

- Wash-away appliqué sheets (*for the turned-edge method*), such as Wash-Away Appliqué Sheets from C&T Publishing (see Resources, page 64)

- Fusible interfacing for lightweight fabrics

- Washable glue in bottle

- Micro tip (for glue bottle) (see Resources, page 64)

- Washable glue stick (*for both the raw-edge and turned-edge methods*) (see Glue Down Appliqués, at right, and Back-to-School Sales, at right)

- Wax paper

- Pressing cloth

SUPPLY TIPS

STAY ORGANIZED

It helps to stay organized, especially when working with designs containing multiple shapes and fabrics. I always make an extra photocopy of each design so that I can make notes directly on the copy. I use a key to assign each fabric a letter or number and then note which fabrics I will use in each section.

USING A LIGHTBOX

A lightbox is a valuable tool for quilters. Many different styles of lightboxes are available for the quilting and crafting markets. Appliqué work usually does not require a large surface.

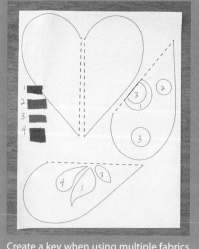

Create a key when using multiple fabrics.

Using a lightbox to provide placement lines for your appliqué shapes, trace the appliqué pattern onto your background fabric with a temporary marking implement.

Put letters or numbers corresponding to your appliqué shapes within the appliqué shape outlines on your background fabric. Some designs contain many small pieces, making it easy to become confused as to which piece fits where.

GLUE DOWN APPLIQUÉS

Adhere appliqué shapes to the background fabric using a temporary adhesive such as washable school glue. With raw-edge appliqué, it is not necessary to overlap shapes. Instead, they can just butt up to one another. This reduces bulk, especially with textured fabrics such as felts and Ultrasuede. Apply glue liberally to the edges of all shapes. Do not skimp on points, as they may lift up during the stitching process.

BACK-TO-SCHOOL SALES

Back-to-school sales are great opportunities to stock up on washable school glue sticks. Store them in airtight containers or sealable plastic bags because they have a tendency to dry out. Do not be afraid to use washable glue in your projects. It dries clear, causes no harm to your machine, and can be washed out if desired. I don't always wash my projects and find that they are plenty soft even when the glue remains in the project.

Raw-Edge Method

With raw-edge appliqué, it is not necessary to add a seam allowance to the edges of the appliqué shapes. Instead, cut each shape from the fabric based on the finished shape and size provided by the pattern, disregarding any seam allowances that may be included. The patterns in this book do *not* include seam allowances.

TIP: Making a Template

Making a plastic appliqué template saves time when cutting out multiple simple shapes. A plastic template provides a nice edge for tracing the pattern onto fabric. Tracing the shapes directly onto the fabric is more accurate than using a pinned paper pattern. Remember to use the not-as-good scissors for creating the plastic templates: The plastic will quickly dull the blade of your good scissors.

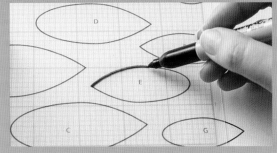

Make templates using appliqué template plastic.

Turned-Edge Method

(USING WASH-AWAY APPLIQUÉ SHEETS)

My preference for working with fabrics that ravel or fray is to turn the edges. I love the clean, crisp effect of turned-edge appliqué. In addition to the aesthetic benefit, the quilt will have a longer life: Threads won't work their way loose.

Wash-away appliqué sheets, such as Wash-Away Appliqué Sheets from C&T Publishing (see Resources, page 64), truly changed my life! Once I learned that I could turn the edges of my fabric onto a fusible, wash-away foundation that I could leave inside my work, the world was at my fingertips. I had previously used methods that required removal, such as the freezer-paper / starch technique. These extra steps lengthened the appliqué process.

Wash-away appliqué sheet foundations remain in your quilt and, with wear and washing, soften into a fiberlike material. I have found that construction manipulation is enough to soften it, so I do not always wash it out.

TIP: Fusible Interfacing

If you are using lightweight fabrics for large, simple appliqué shapes with gradual curves, fusible interfacing can be used as a foundation as an alternative to the wash-away sheets.

TRACING

Trace the appliqué patterns onto the wash-away appliqué sheet with the pattern right side up and the sheet shiny side up. It is important that the shiny, adhesive side of the wash-away sheet be facing up when you trace or copy the appliqué pattern; otherwise, the result will be a mirror image of the intended design. Stay consistent so that the pieces fit together correctly.

It is very important to have the shiny (fusible) side up when tracing the pattern onto the wash-away appliqué sheet.

Always use an erasable pen or pencil to trace the appliqué patterns onto the wash-away appliqué sheet. Permanent ink may stain your fabric. It is not necessary to add a seam allowance to the shape when tracing. The traced shapes on the sheet should be their actual size in the design.

PHOTOCOPYING

Because the wash-away appliqué sheet is like paper, it can be run through an inkjet copy machine. Be sure you know how paper feeds into the printer/copier to ensure that the printing is on the shiny side. Because the sheets tend to stick together, they should be fed into the machine individually and copied one at a time.

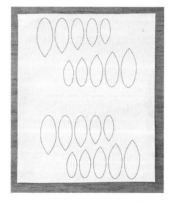

Copy appliqué patterns quickly using an inkjet printer.

TIP: Caution

Do not use fusible wash-away appliqué sheets in a laser printer/copier or any other kind of heat-activated copier!

CUTTING THE WASH-AWAY APPLIQUÉ SHEETS

Cut the foundation shapes from the wash-away appliqué sheets exactly on the marked lines. Keep the cut pieces organized by labeling them on the side that does not get fused down (the nonshiny side). Some patterns are made up of many small shapes. It is easy to lose little pieces if you do not stay organized. I place the labeled, cut appliqué foundations back onto the actual pattern until I am ready to apply them to the fabric.

APPLYING WASH-AWAY APPLIQUÉ SHEETS TO FABRIC

Fuse the appliqué shape foundations onto the *wrong* side of your appliqué fabric with an iron, following the manufacturer's directions for temperature settings and time. Always check that the adhesive (shiny) side is placed down. Place the foundation pieces far enough apart on the fabric to leave room to include a ¼˝ seam allowance around the edges of each of the foundation pieces.

All shapes need a ¼˝ seam allowance for turning.

CUTTING OUT SHAPES

Include a ¼″ seam allowance when cutting around the appliqué foundations. If the shapes include sharp curves, clip the seam allowance to the foundation for ease in turning.

Clip into the seam allowance if shapes contain sharp curves.

TURNING THE EDGES

Use a glue stick to apply washable glue to a wash-away appliqué foundation. Hold the piece so that you are working toward your body as you turn the edges. Use your thumb to press the fabric onto the foundation. The material is firm, so rely on your sense of touch to properly turn the edges. Use your fingertips or nails to distribute areas of fullness, keeping the turned edges smooth.

Apply washable glue to the foundation.

Use your thumb to press the fabric edges onto the foundation.

TIP: Wax Paper

Single sheets of wax paper provide an excellent way to keep your work space clean when working with glue.

Points

WIDE POINTS

Points can be tricky. If a point is wide enough, it is possible to manage turning the edge without clipping at the point.

1. Glue and turn under the fabric on the first side.

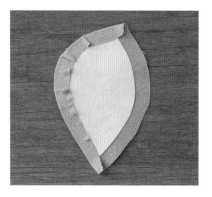

2. Fold and glue at the point so that the second turned edge does not extend beyond the first edge.

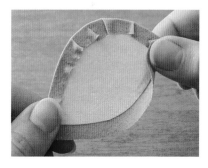

3. Secure the edge past the point with glue.

4. Distribute the fullness using your fingertips or nails.

TIP: Tools for Turning

You may want to invest in a pointy tool for the turning process, such as Alex Anderson's 4-in-1 Essential Sewing Tool from C&T Publishing (see Resources, page 64). Though I prefer to use my fingertips for the tactile benefit, turning tools can assist in distributing fullness.

Distributing fullness with a turning tool

NARROW POINTS

Narrow points usually need to be clipped to some extent, as there is no place for the seam allowance to go.

1. Turn the first edge.

2. Turn the second edge, allowing the seam allowance to extend beyond the first turned edge.

3. Cut away the excess seam allowance.

4. Apply Fray Check to the point.

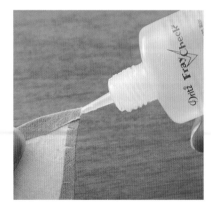

TACKING THE APPLIQUÉ SHAPES TO THE BACKGROUND FABRIC

After the edges have been turned, temporarily attach them to your background fabric using washable liquid glue, beginning with the bottom layer of pieces. If precise design placement is desired, trace the pattern onto the background fabric first, using a temporary marking implement and a lightbox (see Using a Lightbox, page 12).

Attaching a micro tip (see Resources, page 64) to the glue bottle helps control the output of the glue. Apply the glue close to the edges of the appliqué shapes, using liberal amounts, particularly at the points (if applicable).

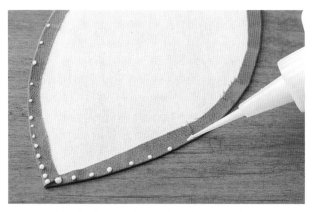

Use washable glue from a glue bottle with a micro tip to temporarily attach the appliqué shapes to the background fabric.

Once the adhesive is dry, you are ready to begin the stitching/quilting process.

Fusible Method

Using a paper-backed fusible web product with fabrics that ravel helps to reduce the raveling somewhat. This method is easy and versatile because the edges remain raw and unturned. There are many different products available. I recommend the more lightweight webs; heavier weights may gum up needles and contribute to skipped stitches. Test different brands and weights until you find your favorites. Always refer to the manufacturer's instructions for iron temperatures and pressing times, as they may vary.

1. Trace the appliqué patterns onto the *paper side* (fusible side should be *down*) of the fusible web with the appliqué pattern *right side down*. (This is important so that you don't end up with a mirror image of the design.) A lightbox (see Using a Lightbox, page 12) is a helpful tool for this tracing process.

2. Leave approximately ½″ between patterns for cutting apart. Label each pattern piece.

3. Cut the pattern pieces apart, leaving a ¼″ seam allowance around each piece.

4. Fuse the patterns to the *wrong* side of the fabric, following the manufacturer's instructions.

5. Cut out the appliqué shapes on the lines.

6. Remove the paper backing and fuse to the *right* side of the background fabric, according to the manufacturer's instructions. Begin with the bottom layer of shapes and overlap where necessary.

Threads for Appli-Quilting

Thread is the final ingredient that brings your quilts to life. It allows you to create magic with your needle. There are so many factors to consider when choosing thread, such as fiber types, weights, manufacturers, and colors. A familiarity with the basics of thread is helpful when it's time to choose the perfect thread for your project.

Some threads are quite easy to use and can hold up under a lot of friction, tension, and fast quilting. However, not all threads are created equal. It is important to recognize that various types of threads behave differently and require different machine settings and quilting speeds. With the right setup, you should be able to use any thread you like.

Types

COTTON

Cotton thread is a great choice for quilters who prefer to use natural fibers in their work. Cotton provides a matte finish, which is sometimes preferred over a shiny finish. It tends to produce lint, which means that your machine needs to be cleaned frequently when it is used. (The better the thread quality, the less lint produced.) Cotton is quite durable and washes and wears wonderfully. When I create utility quilts, especially those intended for children, I use cotton thread because it holds up under multiple wash and dry cycles.

POLYESTER

Polyester is a synthetic fiber that produces a brilliant luster. Polyester thread is strong and easy to work with, and it wears well over time. I use polyester threads frequently because they are quite reliable and give my stitching a fancy, custom look.

METALLIC

Metallic thread offers dramatic visual impact. I love to emphasize design elements by using small doses of metallic thread, adding a touch of glitz to the right project. Metallic thread is quite delicate and tends to be persnickety. Nevertheless, with the right tension setting, needle size, and bobbin thread and slower sewing speeds, it can be used with minimal breakage.

SILK

Silk, like cotton, is a natural fiber. It is very luxurious and provides a high-quality look and feel to your work. For many years, silk was the only type of thread available in 100-weight. It quickly became my favorite choice for precision work and show quilting because it was beautiful and allowed me to quilt intricately. It is surprisingly strong and durable. When sewn at slower speeds, silk thread can be used with success and minimal breakage.

NYLON INVISIBLE

Invisible thread is a must-have for invisible appliqué. The thread will be concealed on both the appliqué shapes and the background fabric. I prefer nylon to polyester for this purpose because nylon lacks the shine that polyester produces. Nylon invisible thread is also very fine, whereas polyester invisible thread tends to feel like fishing line. I have heard some concerns expressed about nylon threads having low melting temperatures; in all the years that I have been using it, however, I have never encountered any issues with melting. Though it is available in both smoke (for darker-colored fabrics) and clear, I find that the clear works perfectly for all fabric shades.

Weight

A thread's weight indicates how heavy or fine it is. Remember, the larger the number, the finer the weight; the smaller the number, the heavier the weight. Threads with a small number, such as 10-weight, may be too thick to fit through the eye of a needle. These threads can still make an appearance on your quilt; they just need to be applied through the bobbin, as shown in Bobbin Work (page 43). Choose a thread's weight based on the look you want to achieve and the style of stitching you are using.

A 30-weight polyester thread is a great choice for blanket stitches, in which the edge is triple stitched, as in *Fractured Leaves* (page 7). The stitch buildup combined with the heavier weight emphasizes the appliqué shape.

A 100-weight silk thread is the perfect choice for intricate designs, such as those found in *A Touch of Red* (page 48). The thread does not build up and allows the pattern of the design to shine.

Although 8-weight decorative threads are too thick to fit through the eye of a needle, they create a fabulous effect in bobbin work—stitching on the reverse side of a quilt with the decorative thread in the bobbin.

Bobbin Thread

Unless I am doing bobbin work, I always use fine (50- to 60-weight) polyester thread in the bobbin. It does not produce lint and blends beautifully with my top threads. Good stitch quality is much easier to achieve using the finer-weight polyester bobbin threads. In addition, bobbins hold much more yardage with the finer-weight thread. This means more quilting time and less time spent stopping to change bobbins. My preference is for prewound bobbins. I find that they are a worthwhile investment, as time is saved not having to wind each bobbin. I do not match my bobbin color to my top thread color. Instead, I blend them. Blending the threads using neutral colors in the bobbin works well and allows me to stock up on fewer colors of prewound bobbins. I am always amazed at how well the colors blend and pleased about how easy the process becomes. I used to wind each and every bobbin using the top thread. It was always difficult to predict how many bobbins I would need: Often I either had to unthread my machine to wind a new bobbin or ended up with half-filled bobbins that I rarely used up.

BLENDING WARM-COLORED THREADS

Warm thread colors

Warm-colored top threads, such as reds, oranges, and golds, blend beautifully with brown bobbin threads. If you use a lot of warm tones in your quilting, I suggest keeping three or four different shades of brown bobbin thread on hand. Choose three or four very different shades in light, medium, and dark values. Always pull the threads away from the spool to test that the shades are similar.

Blending neutral brown bobbin thread with warm top thread colors

BLENDING COOL-COLORED THREADS

Cool-colored threads

Cool-colored top threads, such as purples, pinks, and blues, blend well with gray bobbin threads. If you enjoy using cool colors on the top, invest in three or four shades of gray bobbin thread. I recommend a light, a dark, and two medium shades.

Blending neutral gray-colored bobbin thread with cool top thread colors

IN-BETWEEN COLORS

Depending on the tone, certain colors may read as either warm or cool. For example, greens and mauves/purples that contain large amounts of blue tend to read as cool colors. I like to keep a few shades of taupe thread on hand for the colors that are difficult to read. Taupe is a combination of brown and gray, so it tends to blend well with challenging colors.

Tricky-to-read top thread colors with taupe bobbin thread colors

Needles

Stock up on needles of many different sizes. For longarm users, MR 3.0–MR 5.0 is a good range; for domestic machine users, 10–18 is a good range. For domestic machine users, I recommend using either embroidery or topstitch needles because their larger eyes reduce thread fraying and breakage. I change my needle frequently, after about six hours of quilting time.

When using a heavy thread, you may need to use a larger needle, such as an MR 5.0 or 18. Larger needles have larger eyes, which means there is less friction on the thread. It is good to stitch delicate threads using smaller needles, such as MR 3.0 or 10. If you find, however, that the thread is continually breaking, troubleshoot by changing to a larger needle with a larger eye. This change should be made in small increments. For example, if you are having trouble with a size 10 needle, try a 12.

Small needles should not be used when very fast stitching is going to take place, because they can bend and damage the bobbin hook or throw off timing with longarm machines. With that caveat, I always select the smallest needle appropriate for the job because smaller needles produce smaller holes in the quilt.

Tension

Once I tackled understanding tension, my quilting world seemed larger—as did the selection of threads that I was able to use successfully. I wanted to share this great understanding, so I came up with an arm-wrestling analogy that seems to really help quilters make sense of a difficult and sometimes frustrating concept.

ARM-WRESTLING ANALOGY

Balanced tension

Low needle thread tension or high bobbin thread tension

High needle thread tension or low bobbin thread tension

When setting tension, imagine an arm-wrestling match in which the opponents should be matched in strength. One opponent is the bobbin thread (BOB); the other opponent is the top thread (TOM).

Here is the point: There is no winner, ever. When the stitch is beautiful and to your liking, everybody wins. Do not be afraid to make adjustments to your machine tension. For longarmers this may involve simply turning a knob or screw or bypassing tension dials altogether; for home machine users, it involves adjusting the number. Play, experiment, adjust. It's okay—there are no tension police!

Imagine you are viewing the quilt from the top and you observe thread from the bobbin being pulled up to the top, as shown.

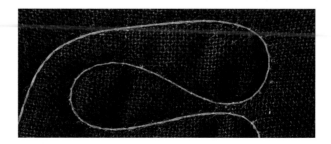

This indicates that TOM is winning; he is much stronger than BOB. The goal is for TOM and BOB to be matched in strength. You need to weaken TOM or strengthen BOB.

This can be done as follows:

- Weaken TOM by reducing the tension. As you make adjustments, pull the thread so that you can feel the effects as the changes are made.

- Strengthen BOB by turning the screw on the bobbin case to the right (think: "righty tighty").

Once you understand tension, you are free to explore and use the fabulous selection of decorative threads available. Specialty threads are often delicate and do not tolerate tight tension settings; they are "weaklings." To be successful when using them, you need to accommodate their needs. Allow them to function as weaklings, reducing TOM's super strength/tension. Then simply match them up with weakling opponents by removing BOB's strength/tension as well.

TIP: Don't Become Limited by the Default

Don't worry about what the tension setting says. If your tension is set at zero and your stitch quality is great, then you have achieved the right setting. Don't become limited by "default" settings; they are suggestions.

TIP: Annotations

As you practice, record your successful settings with particular threads for future reference. This gives you a starting point as to tensions and speeds that have worked for you previously. Different projects may require different settings, but having a point of reference can get you closer at the start.

Troubleshooting

THREAD OBSTACLES

If you have set your tension and achieved a good stitch quality and suddenly things go wrong, chances are there is something else going on. Don't rush to change the settings until you have assessed the situation. If your thread is suddenly breaking, check its path first. Sometimes the thread becomes tangled or wrapped around guides or around the base of the spool holder, which impedes its flow. If you stitch at varied speeds—fast, then slow—you may develop some slack in the thread, which can cause tangles. This is a simple fix: Use a thread net to control the output of thread.

BEWARE OF THE BURR

Sometimes burrs develop in a machine's needle or stitching plate. A *burr* is a subtle ding or imperfection in the metal that cuts your thread as it passes over the burr. With home sewing machines, throat plates can become burred as a result of needle breaks. Needles—even brand-new needles—can have burrs. Feel your machine's throat plate to check for burrs. If they are present, use a file to smooth out the metal. You can check for needle burrs by grabbing the thread from behind and in front of the needle, then moving it around inside the eye. You will quickly notice a burr because it will shred or break your thread. If your needle contains a burr, discard it and replace it with a new one.

MATCH YOUR SPEED TO YOUR THREAD

Speed is a very important factor in thread success. Always think through your project before selecting a thread. If you are working on a utility quilt with very open, large-scale designs that are better quilted at faster speeds, select a stronger utility thread. If your project is intricate, with close, precise stitching, and you are stitching slowly to stay in control, using a delicate thread is appropriate.

Free-Motion Overview

Ergonomics

With the correct ergonomics, you should be able to quilt comfortably for many hours without suffering from sore muscles or fatigue. When learning new designs and techniques, you may have to remind yourself to relax. When you are working on unfamiliar designs, it is easy to concentrate on the execution of shapes and skills and forget to think about your body position.

BODY POSITION

Your shoulders should always be relaxed as you are quilting. Elbow positioning is directly related to shoulder positioning. If your elbows are elevated, your shoulders tighten automatically. Always keep your elbows at your side so that your shoulders can remain relaxed. It is also important that you keep your body in line with the needle. If you position yourself to one side of the needle, your spine will be out of line while you work and you will become sore and tired quickly.

VISUAL PREFERENCES

All quilters have different visual requirements. Some require a shorter distance from the needle when performing intricate work, while others prefer a bit more distance. Larger-scale designs create different preferences. I use a chair with adjustable heights for both longarm and domestic machine quilting so that I can select the right visual distances based on my projects and adjust my height accordingly. For longarm quilting, drafting chairs work beautifully. They are a bit taller to accommodate the height of the machines. If you do not place your body close enough to your work, you may find yourself hunching over to get a better view. This inevitably leads to back fatigue and soreness.

> **TIP:** Magnifying Visual Aids
>
> Try magnifying your work when executing precise shapes. You may use magnifying eyeglasses or attach a magnifying glass to the front of your machine.

Speed

The speed at which you move either your quilt (when domestic machine quilting) or your machine (when longarm quilting) should vary based on your design choices. Using appropriate speeds contributes to success with machine quilting. Find your personal "happy speeds" and note them on your samples. Experiment with very open, loose quilting designs at both fast and slow speeds. Perform the same speed tests with smaller designs and record your results. Generally it is easier to execute open designs with faster movements, but it is nearly impossible to maintain the control needed to create tiny, intricate designs when your movements are too fast.

Stitches per Inch

Understanding stitches per inch (SPI) settings will help you achieve success in your quilting. The SPI settings are unlike the stitch-length settings found on domestic machines. Used in stitch regulation with both domestic and longarm machines, SPI refers to the number of stitches per inch. This means that the larger the number, the smaller the stitch length, and vice versa.

Adjust this setting based on the scale of your quilting designs. If your designs are open and large in scale, select a smaller SPI number to produce a longer stitch length. If your designs are intricate and small in scale, select a larger SPI number to produce smaller stitches. Long stitch lengths cannot accommodate tight curves, so they cannot be used to make tiny shapes. Compare the photographs below.

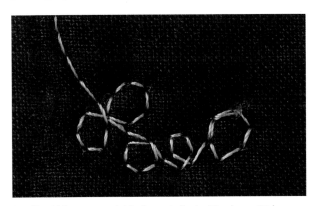

Small pebbles appear rigid when stitched with a long stitch. This example uses SPI 10.

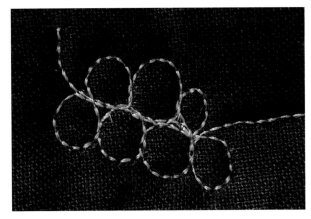

Increasing the SPI to 16 produces better pebbles.

Guiding the Quilt

Always maneuver your quilt top with a light hand. If you place too much weight on your quilt with your hands, the quilt will not move freely. Use a gripping aid so that you don't have to struggle to move the quilt. This way your focus can be placed on fluidity and good design execution. I mainly use my fingertips to guide a quilt, particularly with intricate designs. Many quilters like to wear machine quilting gloves. My preference is for finger cots. I find that finger cots don't inhibit hand movement the way that gloves can. In addition, finger cots do not heat up your hands.

DOMESTIC MACHINE

Supplies

- Sewing machine with free-motion capabilities

- Free-motion quilting foot (also known as a darning or hopping foot)

- Gripping aids, such as gloves or finger cots

Flat, Level Surface

The goal is to lay out your quilt flat at your machine. If you have a large surface, quilting is much easier. Your quilt should be level with your stitching plate so that you are not struggling to maneuver the weight and bulk of the quilt. If you have a large extended base, keep it attached to your machine as you quilt. If you do not have an extended base or drop-in table, elevate the edges of your quilt to reduce drag.

> **TIP:** Use Containers to Elevate Your Quilt
>
> If you do not have a drop-in sewing machine table, elevate the quilt using large, shallow containers.

> **TIP:** Intricate Designs
>
> For intricate designs, place your fingertips fairly close to the needle. Work through the designs using a kneading motion with your fingertips. This soft touch will help you produce delicate stitches while maintaining good control.

LONGARM MACHINE

It is very important to relax when spending time at your longarm machine. Oftentimes people approach the machine with fear and anxiety. Remember to always have a positive and happy attitude when you quilt. Your positivity will carry through to your work!

When learning new techniques, allow yourself time to learn and improve. Track your progress: You will be amazed at how quickly you improve when you practice with a positive outlook!

> **TIP:** Avoid the Death Grip
>
> Remember that longarm quilting is referred to as "hand guiding" not "hand forcing." Avoid gripping the handles with a death grip. Not only does a tight grip lead to fatigue, but it makes it difficult to execute smooth designs.

Stitches

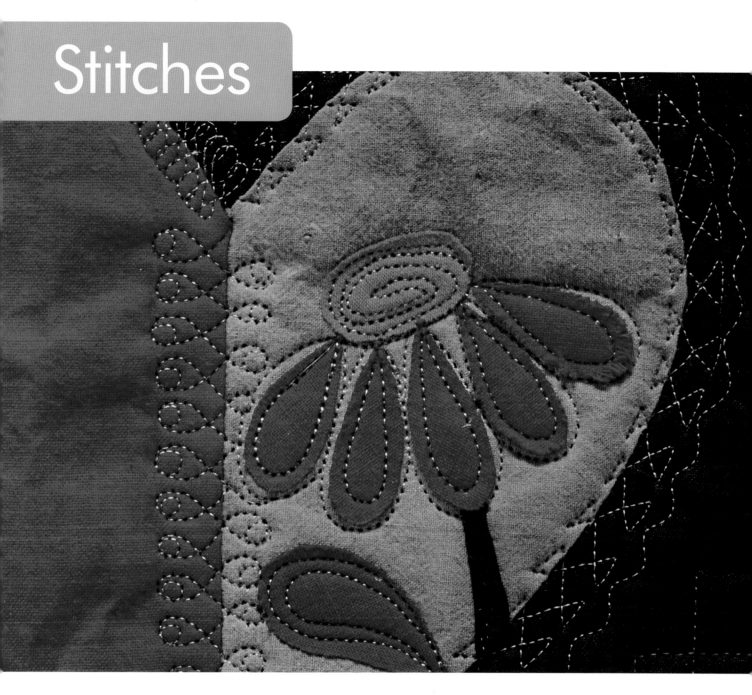

After your quilt top has been pieced (if applicable) and your appliqué shapes are secured, it is time to create your quilt sandwich (for home machines) or load your quilt onto the longarm machine. Now the real fun begins! The stitching is what truly brings the quilt to life. Not only do you begin to see the appliqué shapes come to life by the accenting thread but you see texture develop through the quilting.

The magic of Appli-Quilting happens at your fingertips. This technique does not use programmable decorative stitches. The decorative work comes instead from your imagination. For domestic machines, always disengage the feed dogs, which allows you to move the quilt freely. The beauty of this is that you can move the quilt multidirectionally. Some designs contain little crevices that would require a lot of effort to negotiate if the feed dogs were engaged. Having free range of motion makes this task much easier.

Setup

Most of the stitches discussed in this chapter require a very slow, controlled speed to execute well. I encourage you to try creating these stitches without a regulator, even if you are most comfortable using stitch regulation. The quick directional shifts are difficult for some regulators to read, causing jumped or skipped stitches. I find that it's easier to make fluid movements when the rhythm of the machine is constant. It's best to produce small stitches, 16–18 stitches per inch, to accommodate tight curves. With the slow movement, this should be easy. If you are using a home machine, let off the foot pedal so that your machine won't outrun you. If you are using a longarm machine, set the manual speed to a slower speed, such as 20%–35%. If, after trying Appli-Quilting in manual/constant mode, you decide that you would prefer regulation, set the stitches-per-inch setting to 16 or more.

PRACTICE

It is always good to practice away from the machine prior to stitching. I recommend printing out a copy of your appliqué design and then sliding it into a plastic sheet protector. You now have a makeshift dry-erase board. Audition stitch styles using a dry-erase marker so that you can learn the design and begin to determine good stitching paths, including possibilities for secondary designs (page 38).

Makeshift dry-erase practice sheet

TIP: Helpful Longarm Tool

If you are using a longarm, you may wish to invest in a pushing tool, such as my Control Freak tool, which is a thick acrylic ruler that you hold against the hopping foot. These tools are designed to provide more control but also work well for keeping the appliqué shapes secured.

STITCH ANGLE

Pay attention to the angle of the stitch design. The angle should stay consistent with the edge of the appliqué shapes. As the appliqué shapes curve and shift, adjust the stitching design to match. The majority of the stitches in this chapter use a 90° angle to the edge of the appliqué, though 45° variations can be effective as well. Whichever angle you select, keep it consistent.

TIP: Perfect Points

Slow down at shape tips to ensure that the stitch secures the point. If precision is important, you may choose to use the hand wheel to manually position the needle so that the stitch lands in the intended location.

Traditional Stitches

APPLIQUÉ STITCH

This stitch is a combination of an outline with a "bite" into the appliqué shape. The bite is the stitch that secures the appliqué shape to the background. You can adjust the distance of the bites based on your fabric choice or desired look. If you want the bites spaced farther apart, stitch your outline farther. If you'd like the bites closer together, take fewer stitches for the outline stitch.

I like to use this stitch when I am creating invisible appliqué. I take frequent, tiny bites using nylon invisible thread and a small needle. It is important that the angle of the bite stays at a consistent 90° to the appliqué shape. As the shape curves, adjust the bite so that the angle doesn't become distorted. You now have an outlined and secured appliqué design!

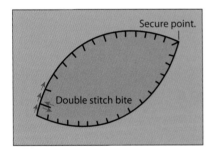

Appliqué stitch. If your appliqué design contains points, position the bite so that the point is secured.

From *Silver Lining* (page 55). The appliqué stitch is an excellent choice for invisible appliqué. Use nylon invisible thread for truly invisible appliqué.

BLANKET STITCH

The blanket stitch is very similar to the appliqué stitch except that the outline portion of the stitch is triple-stitched to emphasize the edge of the appliqué shape.

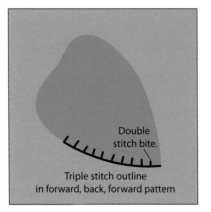

Blanket stitch

Detail of *Winter Wonderland* pillow. Experiment with contrasting threads when using blanket stitches. The effect can really draw attention to the appliqué design.

Winter Wonderland pillow

ZIGZAG STITCH

The zigzag stitch has been used since the beginning of sewing! It is simply a combination of stitches at a 45° angle to the appliqué edge, reflecting as they build. You can get different effects based on the width of the zigzag. A tiny stitch is much less obvious but still secures the appliqué, whereas a larger stitch is more dynamic. You may also wish to experiment with stitch placement. For example, you may want the majority of your stitch to extend outside of the appliqué.

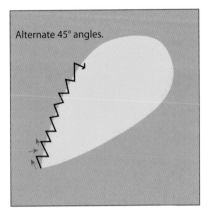

Zigzag stitch (basic)

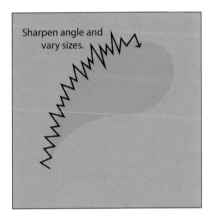

Create a unique variation by combining irregular widths and spacing.

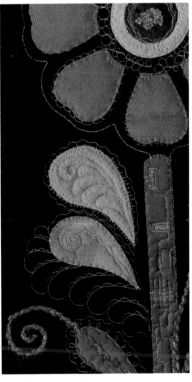

Detail of *Garden Bling* (page 32). This zigzag stitch extends out into the background fabric.

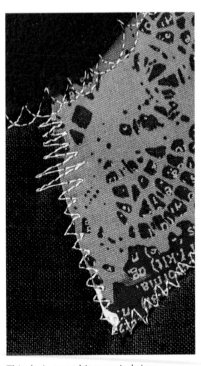

This design combines varied zigzag widths and styles.

INNER OUTLINE STITCH

This stitch is an inner echo of the appliqué shape. I try to stay about ⅛″ away from the edge. If you are too close to the edge, it can be easy to fall off completely. This stitch can be stitched at faster speeds than the other stitches, especially if the designs are large. Since there are fewer directional shifts, you may find it easier to stay in control when moving more quickly.

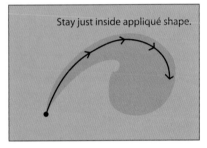

Inner outline stitch

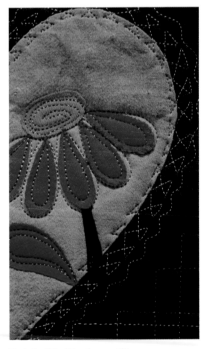

Detail of *Smitten* (page 51)

Nontraditional Stitches

WAVY STITCH

This is an incredibly versatile stitch. It can be simple or elaborate, based on the density and width of the stitch. An open, back-and-forth wavy motion that is very narrow secures the appliqué nicely without overtaking the design.

If you'd like the stitching to be an integral part of the design, create more density by condensing the stitch and widening it so that more of the thread is visible.

You can also achieve a ribbon-candy effect by slightly altering the design so that the waves close on alternating sides.

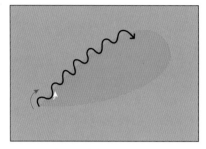

Wavy stitch (simple)

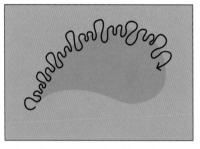

Adjust the density and width of the wavy stitch for more flair.

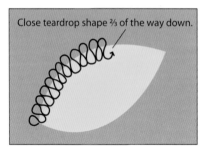

Close teardrop shape ⅔ of the way down.

Ribbon-candy effect

Detail of *Radiant Roses* (page 61). The ribbon-candy effect is a bit more complex but worth mastering.

SCALLOP STITCH

Scallop stitches add a whimsical feel to your work. The peak of the scallop can extend into the background fabric for added dimension, while the valley of the scallop can bite into the appliqué shape to secure it. Experiment and play with fun variations!

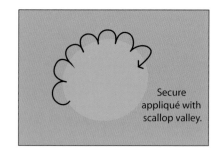

Secure appliqué with scallop valley.

Scallop stitch (basic)

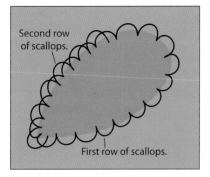

After stitching the first scallop, add a second layer.

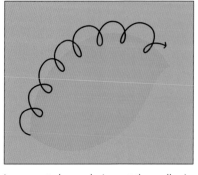

Incorporate loopy designs at the scallop's valleys.

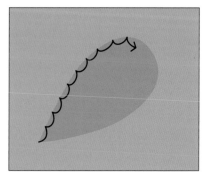

Reverse the scallop so that the peak of the scallop is inside the appliqué shape.

Detail of *Garden Bling*. Double scallop stitch

Garden Bling

DINOSAUR-BACK STITCH

This stitch is very similar to the scallop stitch. The difference is that the peak comes to a point. This simple alteration shifts the stitch's style from whimsical to modern.

FEATHER STITCH

The center of this stitch is at the edge of the appliqué shape. The design is built by adding double stitched lines fanning out at a 45° angle on either side of the appliqué edge. This design is very effective for adding direction.

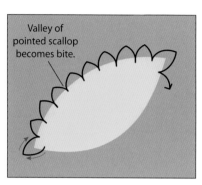

Dinosaur-back stitch

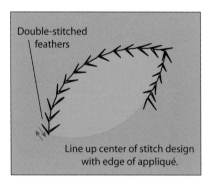

Feather stitch

The feather stitch is great for emphasizing direction. Play with the positioning of the stitch as shown, working from the base of the design toward the tip. Then, reflect that direction on the opposite side.

TIP: Pay Attention to Direction

To emphasize direction and shape, begin at the base of the design and then work toward the tip. When you reach the tip, clip your threads. Begin again at the base of the opposite side, maintaining direction.

FIGURE-EIGHT STITCH

To create this stitch, imagine a zigzag design connected by teardrop shapes. Center the zigzag on the edge of the appliqué shape, allowing the teardrops to alternate from inside the appliqué shape to the background fabric.

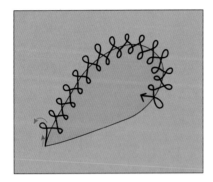

Figure-eight stitch

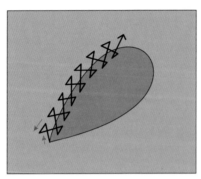

This variation replaces the teardrop shapes with triangular shapes.

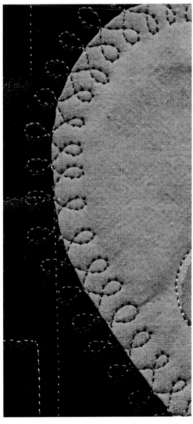

Detail of *Smitten* (page 51). Figure-eight stitch

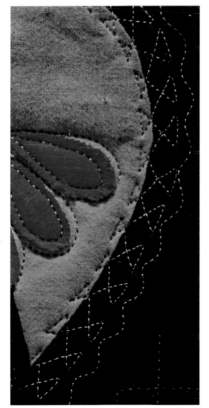

Detail of *Smitten* (page 51). Geometric figure-eight variation

CURLY Q STITCH

Curly Q designs are wonderful! I find that I frequently use them in my quilting, and Appli-Quilting is no exception. Like the feather stitch, this stitch can also be used to emphasize direction. Experiment with size and placement for different effects.

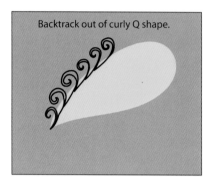

Curly Q stitch

Detail of *Smitten* (page 51). Wide Curly Q stitching is very whimsical. Mirror-image the Curly Q design inside the appliqué for added variety.

"ℓ's AND e's" STITCH

For this stitch design, I think back to my grammar school days, when I learned cursive ℓ's and e's. Experiment with angle placement: 90° and 45° angles are both effective. Develop patterns, if desired: ℓ,e,ℓ,e ... or ... ℓ,e,e,ℓ,e,e,ℓ ...

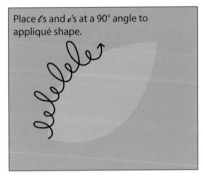

The ℓ's and e's at a 90° angle.

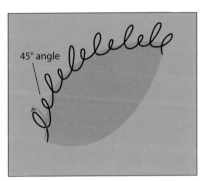

The ℓ's and e's at a 45° angle.

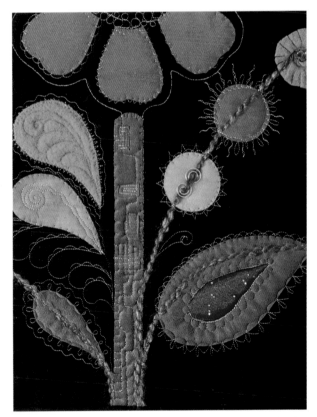

Detail of *Garden Bling* (page 32). Combine ℓ's with dinosaur-back stitching.

Detail of *Garden Bling* (page 32). To create a starburst effect, alternate ℓ's with outward double-stitched wavy lines.

Stitching Paths and Secondary Designs

One of the great features of Appli-Quilting is the ability to add secondary designs and accents to your appliqué shapes. Because you are set up for and in the process of free-motion quilting, you can connect your appliqué shapes through additional quilting designs.

Maintaining Balance

Sometimes appliqué projects present challenges in maintaining balance. As in all quilting projects, it is important to think about balance. For example, if an appliqué shape is very large, incorporate quilting within the actual shape in order to maintain balance. Think about the theme and style of

your quilt when selecting designs to balance out the quilting. Oftentimes simplicity is best and does not detract from the designs. At other times, quilting can build upon the appliqué theme.

Detail of *Smitten* (page 51). Large, open appliqué sections may require additional quilting to maintain balance.

Detail of *Garden Bling* (page 32). Some designs are open to further theme and style development with a second layer … the quilting!

Echoing the Appliqué Designs

Create temporary echo markings using erasable pens or pencils. Incorporate stitching within the echo lines. You may choose to create your appliqué stitch as you work inside the echo by securing the appliqué shapes simultaneously. This dense stitching right along the appliqué design really showcases your work!

You may choose to secure the appliqué as you work within a temporarily marked echo.

Secondary Designs

There are many quilting designs that can be incorporated into your quilting spaces. Quilting provides an added dimension and second layer for both texture and visual appeal. Experiment with your favorites, staying consistent with the style of your quilt and appliqué designs.

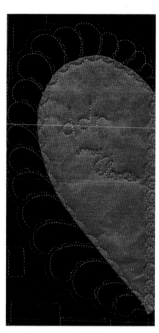

Detail of *Smitten* (page 51) The feathers extending into the background fabric add a whimsical effect while simultaneously securing the appliqué shape. An added reverse scallop completes the design.

EXTENDING THE APPLIQUÉ DESIGNS INTO THE BACKGROUND

This technique adds great dimension and a cohesive quality to the overall design. It requires tracing paper or a water-soluble stabilizer, such as Sulky Solvy (see Resources, page 64). Solvy is my preference because it is very easy to remove and stitch through. If small bits of Solvy remain inside tight stitching, they can be spritzed for quick removal.

1. Use an erasable pen or pencil to trace the appliquéd shapes on the quilt top onto tracing paper or water-soluble stabilizer.

Trace the designs onto tracing paper or water-soluble stabilizer.

2. Pin the traced designs over the background sections and then stitch directly through the product.

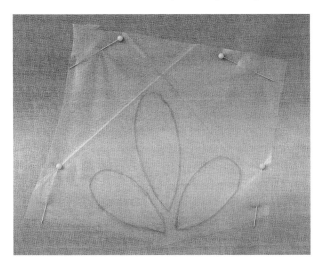

Pin onto the background fabric and then quilt.

3. Remove the paper or stabilizer.

Detail of *Modern Meadow* (page 46). Finished design with product removed

Stitching Paths

Plan your stitching paths ahead of time to minimize stops and starts. Once you have completed your appliqué stitching, travel to another starting point via additional quilting designs.

If you have repeated shapes that return to a center, such as a flower, begin your appliqué stitching at the center. This way, as you work around the petal, you end up at the center and can move on to the next petal with minimal travel stitches.

Detail of *Garden Bling* (page 32). Stitch smart to minimize stops and starts.

Couching and Bobbin Work

Collect yarns and fibers to add to your quilts.

A great way to enhance your projects is by couching fibers onto them. *Couching* is a technique that involves securing fibers, yarns, and so on to a background piece by stitching over them with a decorative or utility stitch. Typically, threads and fibers too thick to fit through the eye of a needle are couched to add texture and dimension to your work. Couching can be executed beautifully using either a longarm or home machine. Through couching you can add unlimited colors and textures to your projects.

Couching

COUCHING FIBER SELECTION

Yarn and Fibers

Yarn comes in a large variety of textures, colors, and thicknesses. As the popularity of knitting has grown, so has the availability of beautiful yarns. Visit local yarn shops or craft stores to add to your stash of couching fibers.

Wool Roving

Wool roving adds a very unique texture to your work. You can stretch and twist it to create interesting shapes and add movement to your project.

Fabric Strips

Very thin fabric strips twisted together can emulate branches and add a wonderful texture to art or landscape quilts. Raveling only enhances the charm of this addition: The more fraying, the better! To encourage raveling, wash and tear small strips.

Thin strips of torn, raveling fabrics can be manipulated for couching.

For a branchlike effect, twist fabrics and then secure them with open couching stitches.

Ribbon and Rickrack

Ribbons and rickrack add a neat dimension. They do not curve well, so it is easiest to use them for straight edges.

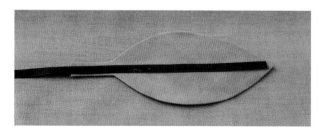

Use ribbons or rickrack for straight design edges.

TIP: Designs with Curves

If your design contains curves, use fusible bias tape to create an effect similar to that of using ribbon and rickrack.

COUCHING STITCH SELECTION

Determine the stitch design you'd like to incorporate based on the amount of texture you desire. A more open stitch design results in more texture because the fibers are simply tacked down with loose stitches rather than flattened with dense stitches.

Zigzag Stitch in Couching

The zigzag stitch (page 30) can take on many different styles, from very traditional to extremely bold and modern. This stitch is quite versatile and is wonderful in its nondescript characteristics. It allows the fibers to play the starring role.

Wavy Stitch in Couching

An open wavy stitch (page 31) is simple and versatile when used for couching. Experiment with varied widths for different effects.

Detail of *Fractured Leaves* (page 7). An open, wavy line is a great choice for couching.

Ribbon-Candy Stitch in Couching

This stitch is very whimsical and tends to be somewhat dense. Imagine a condensed wavy stitch (page 31) that comes to a point and is then mirror imaged. The ribbon-candy stitch is a lot of fun to stitch once you find your rhythm. Move the machine slowly to execute this design and remain in control.

Since the ribbon-candy stitch can be dense, it flattens the fibers somewhat. This makes it excellent for stitching over ribbon or rickrack, neither of which contains much texture.

The ribbon-candy stitch adds a bit of whimsy and is excellent for stitching over ribbon or rickrack.

COUCHING TECHNIQUES

Hand-Guided

1. Mark the design that you would like to add couched fibers over, using an air-erasable marking pen.

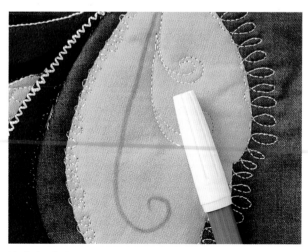

Mark the design.

2. Beginning at the base of the design, place the yarn or fiber directly over the marking, extending beyond the marking.

3. Set the machine so that the stitches end with the needle in the down position.

4. Place the hopping/darning/free-motion foot over the fiber. Pull the fiber tight, front to back. Secure the fiber with 3 small stitches placed individually using the single stitch button. The needle should be holding your place in the down position.

If you are using the stitch regulator, set the stitches-per-inch adjustment to 14 SPI.

5. With one hand, guide the fiber over the marked design. With the other hand, guide the machine or quilt sandwich to stitch the fiber down.

Glue-Tacked

1. Using an air erasable pen, mark the design over which you would like to add couched fabrics.

2. Using washable school glue with a micro tip attached to the bottle, apply glue to the marked design approximately 6″ at a time.

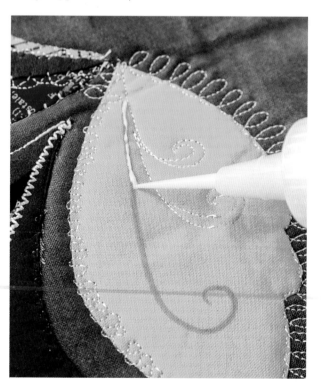

3. Secure the fibers over the glue. Allow 10 minutes to set.

4. Place the machine quilting foot over the fiber carefully so that it doesn't become detached.

5. Place your needle into the fiber to secure the starting point. If you are using a stitch regulator, set your stitches-per-inch setting to 14 SPI.

6. Slowly couch the fiber using the desired stitch design.

TIP: Avoid Pulling Fibers

Do not pull or stretch the fibers as you stitch them down. This causes the background to pucker.

Bobbin Work

Some decorative threads that are too heavy to thread through the eye of a needle can still be used in the bobbin. Heavy threads can be wound onto bobbins either manually or by machine, and they can be used with both longarm and domestic machines.

Decorative threads

STITCHING FROM THE BACK

With bobbin work, you stitch on the reverse side of your quilt. Therefore, you stitch blindly. I like to do the bobbin work last because I can use my initial quilting lines as a shape indicator. If you plan to incorporate bobbin work, plan ahead by selecting a backing fabric that reads as a solid. It makes it easier to see the quilting, giving you a clear path of where to stitch.

Almost-solid backing fabric makes bobbin work easier.

OUTLINING APPLIQUÉ SHAPES WITH DECORATIVE BOBBIN WORK

You can create beautiful effects by outlining appliqué shapes with bobbin work!

1. On the *top* of your quilt, use an Appli-Quilting stitch (see Stitches, page 27) that provides an outline. Use precision when completing this task: The outline needs to be accurate; it will be your guide in the next step.

Use a stitch that outlines the edges of the appliqué shapes.

2. Flip your quilt upside down. Using a decorative or heavy thread in the bobbin, stitch directly on the outline of your appliqué stitch from Step 1. Because you are stitching on the reverse side of the quilt, check the tension and stitch quality ahead of time (see Top Thread and Tension, at right, and Testing for Good Stitch Quality, at right).

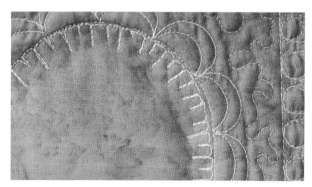

On the reverse side of the quilt, stitch over the appliqué stitch with heavy or decorative bobbin thread.

The result is visually spectacular!

TIP: Top Thread and Tension

Select a top thread strong enough to withstand the tight tension setting needed to secure the heavy bobbin thread to the fabric (see Threads for Appli-Quilting, page 18). I like to use a color that matches the bobbin thread. Invisible thread is also a good choice; it is strong and doesn't show.

TIP: Stopping and Starting

Avoid securing stitches with bobbin work because the heavy thread will appear "built up." Instead, pull the bobbin thread up when you begin and then tie the top thread and bobbin thread in a knot. Dab the knot with a Fray-Check product.

TIP: Testing for Good Stitch Quality

Since you will be working on the reverse side of the quilt, test your stitch quality in advance. When testing tension and stitch quality, use a multidirectional design and varied speeds. It is at the directional shifts that imperfections show up.

When testing for good stitch quality, use a multidirectional design.

PROJECTS

Modern Meadow

FINISHED QUILT: 15½″ × 34½″

MATERIALS

Note: Yardage calculated with 42″ usable width of fabric. (WOF = width of fabric)

- Gray felted wool: 5″ × 9″
- Teal Ultrasuede: 4″ × 5″
- Gray gradation: ½ yard
- Gold solid: 7½″ × 9″
- Purple print: 5½″ × 5½″
- Assorted multicolor prints: 3 strips 1″ × WOF and approximately 10″ × 10″ total of scraps
- ¼″ black fusible bias tape: 4 yards
- Backing: ⅔ yard
- Binding: ⅓ yard
- Batting: ⅔ yard

Additional Supplies

- 2 wash-away appliqué sheets (such as Wash-Away Appliqué Sheets by C&T Publishing) 8½″ × 11″
- Washable glue stick
- Washable glue with micro tip attachment on bottle

CUTTING

Refer to Preparing the Shapes (page 11).

Use the Modern Meadow patterns (pullout page P4).

Gray felted wool

Cut 2 each of pattern pieces I and J.

Cut 1 each of pattern pieces A, D, K, and Q.

Teal Ultrasuede

Cut 1 each of pattern pieces F, G, H, and N.

Gray gradation

Cut 1 rectangle 16″ × 35″ for the background.

Binding

Cut 3 strips 2½″ × WOF.

MODERN MEADOW is a great project that allows you to explore the variety of techniques in this book. It uses both raw- and turned-edge methods and an array of unique fabrics!

Construction

APPLIQUÉ PREPARATION

Refer to Preparing the Shapes (page 11).

Use the Modern Meadow patterns (pullout page P4).

This project uses both the turned-edge method (page 13) and the raw-edge method (page 13).

Wash-Away Appliqué Sheets

1. Trace 1 each of appliqué patterns B, C, F, I, M, O, P, R and S onto wash-away appliqué sheets with the shiny (fusible) side up and the pattern *right* side up. Label the pattern letters on the nonshiny (nonfusible) side.

2. Cut out the appliqué foundations.

Preparing the Turned-Edge Appliqué

1. Fuse or glue wash-away appliqué foundations to the wrong side of the following fabrics, leaving a ¼" seam allowance:

- Gold solid: pattern piece L
- Purple print: pattern piece M
- Multicolor print scrap: pattern piece E

2. Arrange the remaining wash-away appliqué foundations on the remaining fabrics as desired.

3. Cut the appliqué pieces from the fabrics, with a ¼" seam allowance. Turn the edges.

ASSEMBLING THE LEAF DESIGNS

1. Trace the appliqué placement (pullout page P4) for the 3 leaf/stems onto the gray gradation background.

2. Build the designs, beginning with the bottom shapes and overlapping where necessary. Use washable glue with a micro tip attachment on the bottle to adhere the appliqué shapes to the background fabric. Apply glue in a thin bead close to the edges, using liberal amounts at the points.

3. Cut 3 strips from the fusible bias tape for the stems. (You will use the leftover bias tape as dividing strips.) Fuse or glue the bias stems in place.

ADDING THE DIVIDING STRIPS

1. If a turned edge, as shown here, is desired, turn under ¼" on the long edges of the 1"-wide assorted print strips.

2. Cut a strip in half through the width to yield 2 short strips.

3. Fuse or glue the strips in place, combining them with the remaining bias strips in a woven pattern. Refer to the appliqué placement (pullout page P4) for placement.

Quilt assembly

FINISHING

1. Layer the quilt top, batting, and backing, or load onto a longarm machine.

2. Using your chosen stitch designs (see Stitches, page 27), stitch down all the appliqué designs, bias strips, and fabric strips.

> **QUILTING TIPS:** *Modern Meadow*
>
> - Since this project uses both raw-edge and turned-edge methods, you can vary the stitches for added interest and design exploration.
>
> - Remember to travel from stopping points to new starting points by quilting. Try incorporating some of the appliqué elements into your quilting designs using Solvy (see Extending the Appliqué Designs into the Background, page 38).

3. Bind, using your preferred method.

A Touch of Red

A TOUCH OF RED is an impressive display of gradation fabrics. The light-to-dark gradations and simple color scheme create a dramatic effect!

MATERIALS

Note: Yardage calculated with 42″ usable width of fabric. (WOF = width of fabric)

- Gray gradation: 1½ yards

- Red solid: ⅜ yard

- Black Ultrasuede: 10″ × 30″

- Gold fabric gradations in 5 steps from lightest to darkest:

- Fabric 1 (lightest): 8″ × 12″

- Fabric 2: 9″ × 14

- Fabric 3: 9″ × 14″

- Fabric 4: 8″ × 10″

- Fabric 5 (darkest): 6″ × 8″

- ¼″-wide black fusible bias tape: 1 yard

- Backing: 3 yards

- Binding: ½ yard

- Batting: 1⅓ yards, 90″ wide

Additional Supplies

- Lightbox

- 6 wash-away appliqué sheets (such as Wash-Away Appliqué Sheets by C&T Publishing) 8½″ × 11″

- Washable glue stick

- Washable glue with micro tip attachment on bottle

CUTTING

Gray gradation

Cut 2 panels 14½″ × 40½″.

Cut 2 rectangles 14½″ × 20½″.

Red solid

Cut 4 strips 2½″ × 40½″.

Note: Reserve the remaining red fabric for appliqué circles.

Binding

Cut 5 strips 2½″ × WOF.

Construction

PREPARING THE BACKGROUND

Use ¼″ seam allowances.

1. Refer to the background assembly diagram to sew the 2 gray gradation rectangles 14½″ × 20½″ together at the dark ends, as shown, to form the center panel.

2. Finish the background by sewing the center panel, the 2 gray gradation panels 14½″ × 40½″, and the 4 red solid strips 2½″ × 40½″ together as shown. Press the seams toward the panels.

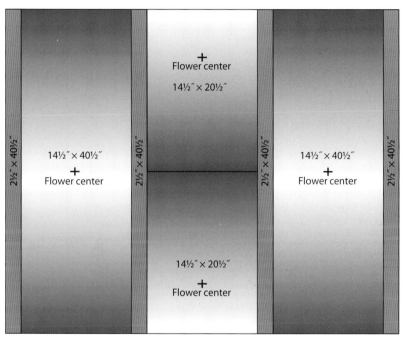

Background assembly

3. Mark the exact centers of the 2 side panels (with the light portion of the gradation in the center), as shown, for the placement of the appliqué flower centers.

4. Then mark the appliqué flower centers on the center panel 6¼″ in from the top and bottom, centered as shown in the background assembly diagram.

5. Using a lightbox, trace the appliqué placement onto the background fabric, referring to the *A Touch of Red* pattern (pullout page P3). Match the marked centers with the flower centers.

APPLIQUÉ PREPARATION

Refer to Preparing the Shapes (page 11).

Use the A Touch of Red patterns (pullout page P3).

This project uses both the turned-edge method (page 13) and the raw-edge method (page 13).

Wash-Away Appliqué Sheets

1. Trace or print the following appliqué designs onto wash-away appliqué sheets with the shiny (fusible) side up and pattern *right* side up. Label each piece on the nonfusible side. Do not add the seam allowance to wash-away appliqué sheets.

- Make 4 of pattern pieces A and J.
- Make 16 each of pattern pieces E, F and G.
- Make 6 of pattern piece H.
- Make 5 of pattern piece I.
- Make 6 of pattern piece K.

2. Cut the foundations out on the line.

Preparing the Turned-Edge Appliqué

1. With the shiny (adhesive) side down, fuse or glue the foundations onto the *wrong* side of the fabrics, leaving a ¼″ seam allowance. Refer to the color placement diagram for appliqué and color placement.

Color placement for appliqué

2. Cut out the shapes, adding a ¼″ seam allowance to the fabric when cutting.

3. Turn the edges, using a washable glue stick (see Turned-Edge Method, page 13).

Preparing the Raw-Edge Appliqué

1. Cut out 16 each of the B, C, and D pattern pieces, as instructed on the pattern pullout page, for raw-edge shapes, or make templates using appliqué template plastic (see Making a Template, page 13).

2. Trace onto Ultrasuede and then cut out directly on the line. Do not add a seam allowance.

3. Layer with turned-edge pieces where applicable, using washable glue in a bottle with a micro tip to secure.

FUSIBLE BIAS TAPE

Add fusible bias tape where applicable onto the appliqué shapes.

BUILDING THE DESIGN ONTO THE BACKGROUND

Build the design, beginning with the bottom layer of shapes. Glue down, using washable glue in a bottle with a micro tip.

FINISHING

1. Layer the quilt top, batting, and backing, or load onto a longarm machine.

2. Refer to Stitches (page 27) to choose a stitch design.

> **QUILTING TIP:**
> *A Touch of Red*
>
> To add flair, experiment with a variety of designs or incorporate red thread!

3. Bind, using your preferred method.

Smitten

MATERIALS

Note: Yardage calculated with 42″ usable width of fabric. (WOF = width of fabric)

- Red solid for pieced strips: 10″ × WOF

- Turquoise solid for pieced strips and appliqué hearts: 15″ × WOF

- Gray solid for background: 1⅛ yards

- Black solid for blocks: ½ yard

- Assorted hand-dyed fabrics for appliqué hearts and details: 6 pieces approximately 4″ × 8″

- Backing: 1½ yards

- Binding: ½ yard

- Batting: 1½ yards, 45″ wide

Additional Supplies

- Lightbox (*optional*)

- 6 wash-away appliqué sheets (such as Wash-Away Appliqué Sheets by C&T Publishing) 8½″ × 11″

- 1 sheet fusible web 8½″ × 11″

- Washable glue stick

- Washable glue with micro tip attachment on bottle

This whimsical quilt combines both raw-edge and turned-edge appliqué. Its design lends itself to stitch exploration, bobbin work, and couching. This is a great project if you want to experiment with different threads, textures, and stitch designs. It's also perfect for including hidden messages for your loved ones in the quilting details.

Red

Cut 3 strips 2½″ × WOF.

Turquoise

Cut 3 strips 2½″ × WOF.
Cut away 2 squares 2½″ × 2½″, and reserve.

Gray

Cut 1 strip 8½″ × WOF; subcut into:

- 1 strip 8½″ × 10½″
- 2 strips 8½″ × 6½″
- 4 strips 8½″ × 4½″

Cut 2 strips 2½″ × WOF; subcut into:

- 1 strip 2½″ × 22½″
- 2 strips 2½″ × 14½″
- 2 strips 2½″ × 8½″

Cut 1 strip 6½″ × 10½″.

Cut 2 strips 4½″ × WOF; subcut into:

- 2 strips 4½″ × 22½″
- 1 strip 4½″ × 12½″
- 1 strip 4½″ × 10½″

Black

Cut 2 strips 8½″ × WOF; subcut into:

- 5 squares 8½″ × 8½″
- 2 strips 8½″ × 4½″

Binding

Cut 4 strips 2½″ × WOF.

Construction

Seam allowances are ¼″.

BLOCK APPLIQUÉ PREPARATION

Refer to Preparing the Shapes (page 11).

Use the Smitten patterns (pullout page P1).

The heart shapes are created using the turned-edge method (page 13). The details of the hearts use the fusible raw-edge method (page 17).

1. Trace the heart patterns onto wash-away appliqué sheets with the shiny (fusible) side up and the pattern *right* side up.

2. Fuse to the wrong side of the fabric, leaving room to include a ¼″ seam allowance.

3. Cut out the shapes, leaving a ¼″ seam allowance for turning.

4. Turn the edges, using a washable glue stick.

5. Using the fusible raw-edge technique, create appliqué detail designs using assorted fabrics.

6. Fuse the details to the heart halves. You may choose to mark the placement guides using a lightbox, or you can just position the designs by eye, referring to the quilt photo (page 51).

QUILT ASSEMBLY

Use ¼″ seam allowances for all piecing.

1. Sew a turquoise and a red 2½″ × WOF strip together lengthwise to make a strip set. Repeat to make a total of 3 strip sets. Press toward the darker fabric. Subcut each strip set into 2½″-wide units for a total of 32 units.

2½″

2. Join 22 units created in Step 1 along the long edges, alternating the color placement to create the checkered strip.

3. Make 2 strips by joining 5 units along the short edges. Add 1 of the reserved 2½″ × 2½″ turquoise squares to the red end of each of these strips, as shown.

Make 2.

4. Refer to the quilt assembly diagram to construct the quilt background, using the appliqué units, pieced strips, and gray fabric as shown.

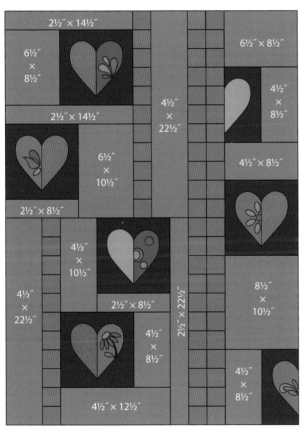

Quilt assembly

FINISHING

1. Layer the quilt top, batting, and backing or load onto a longarm machine.

2. Refer to Stitches (page 27) as needed. Quilt.

QUILTING TIP: *Smitten*

This quilt provides ample negative space for decorative free-motion appliqué stitches. Consider adding hidden messages or words in the quilting to enhance the theme of the quilt.

3. Bind, using your preferred method.

I incorporated bobbin work with heavyweight sparkly threads.

The second colorway for SMITTEN replaces the turquoise and assorted hand-dyed fabrics with scrap fabrics. It uses white fabric in place of gray and pink fabric in place of black.

For my variation, I used only the polka dot appliqué details.

Silver Lining

This delightful wallhanging was inspired by a greeting card. The solid fabrics used provide a gorgeous canvas of negative space for quilt play. You can incorporate appliqué elements into your quilting design for visual interest. I combined many of the techniques explored in this book, including bobbin work; couching; and raw-edge, turned-edge, and fusible appliqué.

MATERIALS

Note: Yardage calculated with 42″ usable width of fabric. (WOF = width of fabric)

- Off-white solid for background: 17″ × 24″
- White for borders: ½ yard
- Green Ultrasuede for leaves and cone trees: 6″ × 7″
- White felt for cloud: 4¾″ × 9½″
- Orange solid for lower tree: 6″ × 8″
- Coral solid for half of upper tree: 4½″ × 9″
- Red solid for half of upper tree: 4½″ × 9″
- Dark red solid for small tree: 4″ × 7″
- Prints for tree trunks: 3 strips 1″ × 11″, 1″ × 14″, and ½″ × 7½″
- Yarn for tree trunks
- Assorted green and aqua scraps for ground:

1 rectangle 2″ × 5″	1 rectangle 3½″ × 4″	1 square 5″ × 5″
1 rectangle 2½″ × 5½″	1 rectangle 3″ × 4″	

- Backing: 1 yard
- Binding: ⅜ yard
- Batting: 1 yard, 45″ wide

Additional Supplies
- 2 wash-away appliqué sheets (such as Wash-Away Appliqué Sheets by C&T Publishing) 8½″ × 11″
- 2 sheets fusible web 8½″ × 11″
- Washable glue stick
- Washable glue with micro tip attachment on bottle
- Bias tape maker (*optional*)

White

Cut 3 strips 4½″ × WOF; subcut into:

- 2 strips 4½″ × 32″
- 2 strips 4½″ × 17″

Binding

Cut 4 strips 2½″ × WOF.

BACKGROUND ASSEMBLY

Use a ¼″ seam allowance.

Attach the white borders to the off-white center as shown in the quilt assembly and appliqué placement diagram.

APPLIQUÉ PREPARATION

Refer to Preparing the Shapes (page 11) as needed.

Use the Silver Lining patterns (pullout page P2).

This project uses the fusible method (page 17), the turned-edge method (page 13), and the raw-edge method (page 13).

If desired, trace the appliqué design placement onto the background using an erasable marking implement.

Preparing the Fusible Appliqué

1. Apply fusible web to the wrong side of the 5 assorted "ground" pieces.

2. Arrange and layer the "ground" pieces onto the background fabric, according to the appliqué placement diagram (next page).

3. When you are happy with the arrangement, fuse down.

Preparing the Turned-Edge Appliqué

1. Trace pattern pieces D, E, G, and H onto wash-away appliqué sheets with the shiny (fusible) side up and the pattern *right* side up. Label the pieces on the nonshiny side.

2. Cut out on the line. *Do not add seam allowances.*

3. Fuse or glue the foundations to the corresponding fabrics, leaving room to add a ¼″ seam allowance around each foundation.

4. Cut out, adding a ¼″ seam allowance around each foundation.

5. Turn the edges, using a washable glue stick. For overlapping trees, it is not necessary to turn the edges of the covered portions.

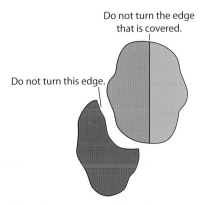

Do not turn the edge that is covered.

Do not turn this edge.

When shapes overlap, it is only necessary to turn the edges on the top piece.

Preparing the Raw-Edge Appliqué

It is not necessary to add a seam allowance for the raw-edge technique.

Cut out shape A from felt and shapes B, C, and F from Ultrasuede. For repeated shapes, you may wish to create a template for tracing using appliqué template plastic (see Making a Template, page 13).

Preparing the Tree Trunks

You may wish to turn the edges of the 1″ × 11″, 1″ × 14″, and ½″ × 7½″ strips used for the larger tree trunks. You can either use an iron to turn ⅛″ under along all edges or use a bias tape maker. If the tops and bottoms of the trunks are exposed, turn those edges as well. Cut yarn to the desired lengths for the smaller tree trunks.

BUILDING THE APPLIQUÉ DESIGN

Build your design beginning with the bottom layer of shapes and ending with the top shapes. Adhere the appliqué shapes to the background using washable glue with a micro tip attachment on the bottle. Use a liberal amount of glue, particularly at points and close to the edges. Refer to Couching (page 40) to glue the yarn tree trunks in place.

FINISHING

1. Layer the quilt top, batting, and backing or load onto a longarm machine.

2. Refer to Stitches (page 27) for stitch design ideas. Quilt.

3. Bind, using your preferred method.

Quilt assembly and appliqué placement

Autumn Tide

FINISHED BLOCKS: A: 24″ × 20″, B: 24″ × 26″
FINISHED QUILT: 56″ × 46″

The simplicity of AUTUMN TIDE's design, combined with the large, felted-wool leaf motifs, makes a bold statement. The appliqué stitches bury nicely into the felted wool, providing a gorgeous texture. The wonderful negative space of this design provides a machine-quilting playground!

MATERIALS

Note: Yardage calculated with 42″ usable width of fabric.
(WOF = width of fabric)

- Teal solid: 1¾ yards
- Navy solid: 1⅓ yards
- Gold solid: ⅓ yard
- Assortment of gold and brown felted wool: 4 pieces approximately 11″ × 14″
- Backing: 3⅛ yards
- Binding: ½ yard
- Batting: 1½ yards, 90″ wide

Additional Supplies
- Washable glue stick
- Washable glue with micro tip attachment on bottle

CUTTING

Teal solid

Cut 2 strips 8½″ × WOF; subcut into:

- 1 strip 8½″ × 26½″
- 1 strip 8½″ × 20½″

Cut 4 strips 6½″ × WOF; subcut into:

- 2 strips 6½″ × 26½″
- 2 strips 6½″ × 24½″

Cut 1 strip 2½″ × WOF; subcut into 2 strips 2½″ × 14½″.

Cut 2 strips 4½″ × WOF; subcut into 2 strips 4½″ × 26½″.

Navy solid

Cut 1 strip 24½″ × WOF; subcut into 4 strips 8½″ × 24½″.

Cut 4 strips 4½″ × WOF; subcut into 4 strips 4½″ × 24½″.

Gold solid

Cut 4 strips 2½″ × WOF; subcut into 4 strips 2½″ × 24½″.

Binding

Cut 6 strips 2½″ × WOF.

Construction

BLOCK ASSEMBLY

Use ¼″ seam allowances.

1. Construct 2 A blocks as shown, pressing the seams toward the dark fabric.

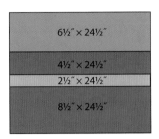

Make 2 A blocks.

2. Construct 2 B blocks as shown, pressing the seams toward the dark fabric.

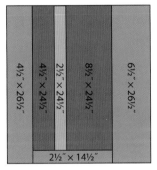

Make 2 B blocks.

APPLIQUÉ PREPARATION

Refer to Preparing the Shapes (page 11).

Use the Autumn Tide patterns (pullout page P1).

The raw-edge method (page 13) is used for all appliqué in this project.

If desired, trace the appliqué design placement onto block sections using an erasable marking implement.

1. Cut out 4 each of the appliqué shapes from the wool assortment. It is not necessary to add a seam allowance.

2. Using washable glue with a micro tip attachment on the bottle, glue the appliqué pieces onto the background fabric. Align the shapes closely rather than overlapping shapes, which would add unnecessary bulk.

QUILT ASSEMBLY

Use ¼″ seam allowances.

1. Sew the A blocks and B blocks together in columns, rotating the blocks to match the orientation shown in the quilt assembly diagram.

2. Sew both 8½″ side strips together at the short ends to make a border strip. Sew the border to the left side of the quilt top.

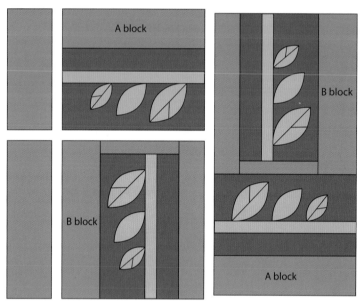

Quilt assembly

FINISHING

1. Layer the quilt top, batting, and backing or load onto a longarm machine.

2. Refer to Stitches (page 27) for stitch selection. Quilt.

3. Bind, using your preferred method.

Radiant Roses

This quilt is both classic and modern. The cotton sateen fabrics really emphasize the elegance of the design.

MATERIALS

Note: Yardage calculated with 42″ usable width of fabric (except for dark brown sateen, which requires a minimum of 43½″ usable width of fabric, or additional yardage to piece strips). (WOF = width of fabric; LOF = length of fabric)

- Dark brown solid cotton sateen: 2 yards

- Turquoise solid cotton sateen: 1¼ yards

- Coral fabric gradations in 6 steps from lightest to darkest:

  Fabric 1 (for pattern pieces A and B): 3″ × 6″

  Fabric 2 (for pattern pieces C, D, E, and F): 5″ × 21″

  Fabric 3 (for pattern pieces G, H, I, and J): 5″ × 32″

  Fabric 4 (for pattern pieces K and L): 8″ × 12″

  Fabric 5 (for pattern pieces M, N, O, and R): 10″ × 50″

  Fabric 6 (for pattern piece S): 8″ × 20″

- Backing: 3½ yards

- Binding: ⅝ yard

- Batting: 1½ yards, 90″ wide

Additional Supplies

- 7 wash-away appliqué sheets 8½″ × 11″ (such as Wash-Away Appliqué Sheets by C&T Publishing) or 1½ yards, 20″ wide

- Fusible interfacing for lightweight fabrics: 2 yards, 20″ wide (not needed if using yardage of wash-away appliqué material)

- Washable glue stick

- Washable glue with micro tip attachment on bottle

Dark brown

Cut 6 strips 4½″ × LOF; subcut into:

- 2 strips 4½″ × 64½″ (borders)
- 4 strips 4½″ × 44½″ (sashing)
- 3 strips 4½″ × 16½″ (block sashing)

Cut 1 strip 16½″ × LOF; subcut into:

- 1 rectangle 16½″ × 32½″
- 1 square 16½″ × 16½″

Turquoise

Cut 3 strips 12½″ × WOF; subcut into 6 rectangles 12½″ × 16½″.

Binding

Cut 7 strips 2½″ × WOF.

Construction

BACKGROUND ASSEMBLY

All seam allowances are ¼″.

1. Refer to the quilt assembly diagram to sew the 16½″-high brown and turquoise rectangles into 3 rows as shown. Press the seams toward the darker fabric.

2. Sew the rows together with the 4 brown 4½″ × 44½″ sashing strips. Press.

3. Sew the 2 brown 4½″ × 64½″ borders to the sides of the quilt top. Press.

4. You may want to mark placement lines for the rose portion of the design. The larger pieces may be positioned by eye.

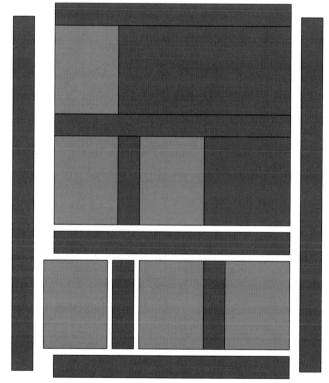

Quilt assembly

APPLIQUÉ PREPARATION

Refer to Preparing the Shapes (page 11).

Use the Radiant Roses patterns (pullout page P1).

The turned-edge method (page 13) is used for all appliqué in this project.

Color and shading play an integral role in the success of this quilt. The highlights are emphasized by the lightest gradation and the shadows by the darkest shade. It is important to keep the fabrics and pattern pieces organized.

Wash-Away Appliqué Sheets

1. Trace or print the following appliqué patterns onto wash-away appliqué sheets with the shiny (adhesive) side up and pattern *right* side up. If you have yardage of wash-away appliqué material, you can also trace the pieces listed under Fusible interfacing (below) now. Label the pattern letters onto the nonshiny (nonfusible) side.

- Make 4 each of pattern piece R.
- Make 3 each of pattern pieces A–L.
- Make 1 each of pattern pieces P, O, Q, and T

2. Cut the foundations out on the line.

Fusible Interfacing

For the rose stems, use fusible interfacing so that you don't have to piece the foundations.

1. Join the upper and lower halves of the M pattern. Trace 1 each of pattern pieces M, N, and O onto fusible interfacing.

2. Cut the appliqué pieces out *directly on the traced line*, as these will be used for turned-edge appliqué.

Preparing the Turned-Edge Appliqué

1. Fuse or glue appliqué foundations and interfacing to the appropriate fabrics on the *wrong* side of the fabric. Leave room to add a ¼″ seam allowance to the sides of the foundations when cutting.

2. Cut out the pieces, including a ¼″ seam allowance for turning.

3. Turn the edges using a washable glue stick.

4. Glue the appliqué shapes to background, using washable glue with a micro tip attachment on the bottle. Refer to the appliqué placement diagram below for placement as needed.

Appliqué placement

FINISHING

1. Layer the quilt top, batting, and backing or load onto a longarm machine.

2. Refer to Stitches (page 27) for stitching designs. Quilt.

3. Bind, using your preferred method.

Resources

THREADS

Superior Threads   superiorthreads.com

Red Rock Threads   redrockthreads.com

TOOLS AND PRODUCTS

The Copper Needle   thecopperneedle.com

GLUE BOTTLE MICRO TIPS

Purple Daisies Quilting   purpledaisiesquilting.com

**WASH-AWAY APPLIQUÉ SHEETS &
ALEX ANDERSON'S 4-IN-1 ESSENTIAL SEWING TOOL**

C&T Publishing   ctpub.com

SOLVY

Sulky of America   sulky.com

**INFORMATION ON
DOMESTIC SEWING MACHINES**

BERNINA   bernina.com

**INFORMATION ON
LONGARM MACHINES**

Innova Longarm   innovalongarm.com

About the Author

Gina Perkes lives in Payson, Arizona, where she owns and operates her quilt shop, training facility, and Innova longarm dealership, The Copper Needle.

Gina learned to quilt in 1998 while expecting her second child. Wanting to make quilts for her children, she took a beginning class at the local quilt shop. Passion quickly ensued. She began entering national quilt shows to feed her competitive drive and improve her skills as an artist and quiltmaker. She has received numerous international and national awards, including the International Quilt Association's (IQA's) Future of the Industry award and the American Quilter's Society's (AQS's) Best Longarm Machine Workmanship award. Her quilt *Nostalgia* now resides at the National Quilt Museum in Paducah, Kentucky, as part of the permanent collection.

Gina is passionate about teaching others and developing patterns and tools for quilters. She has appeared on numerous quilting shows, including *The Quilt Show, Quilt It, iquilt, Linda's Longarm Quilters, Daily Crafts TV*, and *Quilting School*. She travels nationally and internationally to guilds and conferences, teaching her techniques on both domestic and longarm machines.

In 2014, Gina was inducted into the Arizona Quilters Hall of Fame.

Also by Gina Perkes:

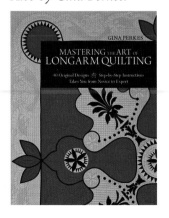